Three Reasons You'll Love

THE
PODCAST
JOURNAL

1. *The Podcast Journal* **has been crafted to give you the right steps at the right time.** No more guessing what's next on your podcasting journey—we'll let you know what your next step is along the way!

2. *The Podcast Journal* **is a proven guide;** these are the exact steps I took to launch the top—ranked business podcast Entrepreneurs On Fire in 2012, along with 10 other podcasts since.

3. *The Podcast Journal* **will hold you accountable.** We're all busy and could be doing any number of other things at any given moment, which is why it's critical to have accountability.

PUBLISHER'S DISCLAIMER

While the publisher and author have used their best efforts in preparing this book, they make no representations or warranties with respect to the accuracy or completeness of the contents of this book. The advice and strategies contained herein may not be suitable for your situation. You should consult with a professional where appropriate. Neither the publisher nor author shall be liable for any loss of profit or any other commercial damages, including but not limited to special, incidental, consequential, or other damages.

ISBN: 978-0-9962340-2-3

Printed in China

Layout by Kate Erickson

Designed by Brandy Thomas

Edited by Stephanie Deveau

Logistics by Richie Norton of Prouduct.com

FIRST EDITION

THE PODCAST JOURNAL

Idea to Launch in 50 Days

John Lee Dumas

ThePodcastJournal.com

TABLE OF CONTENTS

"Keep away from people who try to belittle your ambitions. Small people always do that, but the really great make you feel that you, too, can become great."

— *Mark Twain*

THE IDEA PHASE

Day 1: Mindset

Day 2: Where Does Podcasting Fit?

Day 3: Your Podcast Topic, Part I of III

Day 4: Your Podcast Topic, Part II of III

Day 5: Your Podcast Topic, Part III of III

Day 6: Proof of Concept

Day 7: Confirm Uniqueness

Day 8: Defining Your Avatar, Part I of II

Day 9: Defining Your Avatar, Part II of II

Day 10: Finding Your Avatar

Day 11: Establishing a Connection with Your Avatar

Day 12: Engaging with Your Avatar

Day 13: Your Niche

Day 14: Format, Frequency, and Length

Day 15: Interview or Topic-based Tips

Day 16: Initial Keyword Research

Day 17: Naming Your Podcast

Day 18: Legal Considerations for Your Podcast

Day 19: The Idea Phase Review

THE SETUP PHASE

Day 20: Recommended Equipment

Day 21: Recommended Software

Day 22: Setting Up Your Template and Keyboard Shortcuts

Day 23: Sample Recording and Editing, Part I of II

Day 24: Sample Recording and Editing, Part II of II

Day 25: Exporting and Tagging Your MP3

Day 26: Your Media Host

Day 27: The Setup Phase Review

THE CREATION PHASE

Day 28: Your Podcast Mission Statement

Day 29: Your Podcast Artwork

Day 30: Your Episode Flow

Day 31: Your Podcast Scheduler

Day 32: Your Content's Goal

Day 33: Your Podcast Intro and Outro

Day 34: Recording Episode 000

Day 35: Recording Your First 2 Episodes

Day 36: Editing Your Episodes

Day 37: The Creation Phase Review

THE PRE-LAUNCH PHASE

Day 38: Your Launch Strategy

Day 39: Setting Goals for Launch

Day 40: Your Podcast Website

Day 41: Social Media Presence

Day 42: Your Launch Team

Day 43: Spreading the Word

Day 44: The Pre-Launch Phase Review

THE LAUNCH PHASE

Day 45: Upload and Publish First 3 Episodes

Day 46: Submitting Your RSS Feed

Day 47: Gaining Early Momentum

Day 48: Subscribe, Rate, and Review

Day 49: Ongoing Promotions Checklist

Day 50: Schedule Your 1-Month Podcast Review

WELCOME TO
THE PODCAST JOURNAL

First off: thank you for putting your trust in us! We're so excited you've chosen to start your podcasting journey with *The Podcast Journal*.

Since 2012 we've launched over 10 of our own podcasts, including the top-ranked business podcast Entrepreneurs On Fire. We've also helped guide thousands of other podcasters to launch through our podcasting community, Podcasters' Paradise.

That means the specific steps we've laid out for you to follow over the next 50 days have been proven thousands of times over.

There are a lot of moving pieces and several decisions to be made throughout the process of creating and launching your podcast, and we're here to help guide you every step of the way.

So, let's get started!

GETTING STARTED

Simply by investing in *The Podcast Journal* you've taken the first step towards launching your podcast—congratulations!

Now, the real work begins.

We've laid out exercises and put together all the resources you'll need to go from idea to launch. Trust the process, follow the prompts, and you will launch your podcast in 50 days.

The good news is, it's really that simple.

The challenging news is, it's going to take discipline, focus, and a purpose to help get you to launch, which is why *The Podcast Journal* will be instrumental on your journey.

We've laid out each day to help you focus on the most important steps. With timed exercises and all the recommendations you need to make it happen, launching your podcast is just 50 days away.

We've also put together several resources to help you on your journey, including video tutorials, samples, and templates.

As you go through *The Podcast Journal* you might think about others who are on the same journey as you.

Is anyone else facing the same struggles as me?

Is anyone else wondering whether or not their podcast name, artwork, format, or frequency is what it should be?

The answer is YES. That's why we created our premium podcasting community, Podcasters' Paradise: so you don't have to be alone on your podcasting journey.

What makes Podcasters' Paradise a premium community?

A few things:

- Step-by-step video tutorials to walk you through recording, editing, growing, and monetizing your podcast;
- Recommended tools, services, and resources;
- Email templates and sample documents;
- Monthly live Q&A, guest expert webinars, and
- A private Facebook community where you can ask questions and connect with thousands of other podcasters who are on the same journey as you.

So if you're looking for a community of like-minded people who are on the same journey as you, visit PodcastersParadise.com to learn more.

FAQ

Do the 50 days have to happen consecutively?

If you want to launch your podcast in 50 days, then the days should happen consecutively. But if you have to miss a day, or you have a vacation planned and won't be taking your *Podcast Journal* with you, then pick up where you left off when you can.

What if the exercises in one day take me longer than one day to accomplish?

Everyone has a different schedule and different amounts of time to dedicate to creating their podcast. Don't beat yourself up; stay the course and pick up where you left off the next day—even if that means it takes you two or three days instead of one.

Same goes for the timed exercises you'll see throughout *The Podcast Journal*: the time frame is a recommendation, not a rule.

Where can I go to access my digital pack?

EOFire.com/tpjdigital | password: 7632278 (podcast)

Where can I go to find all of the resources in one place?

EOFire.com/podcastjournal is where you can find every video tutorial, sample, and template we share throughout *The Podcast Journal.*

What happens once I finish my *Podcast Journal*?

Congratulations! When you finish your *Podcast Journal* you'll have launched your very own podcast!

The next step is learning how to grow an audience and monetize, and we cover the top strategies to do just that in our podcasting community, Podcasters' Paradise. Visit PodcastersParadise.com for more details.

Is there a place I can go to meet others who are also using The Podcast Journal to launch their own podcast?

Yes! Join us in our private Facebook group, where those rockin' The Podcast Journal, The Freedom Journal, and The Mastery Journal are all providing guidance and support to one another on their journey! EOFire.com/facebook

Are there other resources that can help me on my podcasting journey?

Yes! We've already mentioned Podcasters' Paradise, and we also have a free video series called Free Podcast Course that also focuses on how to launch your podcast. You can claim your spot today at FreePodcastCourse.com!

The
IDEA PHASE

"Whatever the mind can conceive and believe, it can achieve."

— Napoleon Hill

DAY 1
Mindset

Creating and growing a podcast is a marathon, not a sprint. This is not a get-rich-quick strategy or an easy path to take. In order to set yourself up for success on your podcasting journey, it's important that you:

1. Prepare mentally for what's ahead, and

2. Commit fully to your journey.

EXERCISE:
How to Prepare Mentally for What's Ahead

 Set a timer for 10 minutes

Why do I want to create a podcast?

to hear my voice and have a place to speak my passions

More often than not we come up with what I like to call "surface why's." They might be reasons why you're creating your podcast, but they aren't THE reason why.

If you're feeling a little stuck, a recommended resource for this exercise is Simon Sinek's Ted Talk: Start with Why.

 Set a timer for 15 minutes

Now it's time to dive deeper.

Why do I REALLY want to create a podcast?

for close out there who are in

When you're able to dive so deep into your WHY that you've got it down to 1 sentence or less, write it down here AND on a loose piece of paper.

My WHY for creating a podcast:

Then, tape your WHY somewhere so that you'll see it daily.

Knowing your WHY is important on your podcasting journey because it will help you prepare mentally for what's ahead. When you hit a rough spot, get frustrated by what seems like a lack of progress, or you feel like giving up, remind yourself of your WHY for strength, encouragement, and motivation.

EXERCISE:
Committing Fully to Your Journey

Now that you know your WHY and you've done a little mental preparation for what's ahead, it's time to commit fully to your podcasting journey.

The most successful podcasters in the world are those who:

☐ Know their audience

☐ Create valuable content based on their audience's wants and needs

☐ Are consistent with their craft

☐ Are willing to adapt

☐ Are willing to embrace the journey

Checking all the boxes above isn't easy. Knowing your audience takes a lot of time, because who you think your audience is—and who they might end up being—could be different.

Creating valuable content is hard work—you might do it for months only to find out what you've been creating isn't in line with whom you're attracting.

Being consistent takes discipline. If you're not able to create consistent content for your audience, then there are hundreds of other opportunities out there for them. Give them a reason to continue coming back to YOU.

You have to be willing to adapt. Your audience, the medium of podcasting, and any other number of variables could also change over time.

And finally, you have to embrace the journey—both the ups, the downs, and the in-betweens. It's the only way you'll WIN.

There are going to be a lot of very frustrating moments. It's going to sometimes feel as though growing your podcasting audience is taking FOREVER. It might be a year (or more) before you ever monetize your podcast.

Are you ready to commit fully to your podcasting journey?

Then declare it and OWN it.

Here, and on the same sheet of paper you used to write out your WHY, write down your commitment to your podcasting journey.

My commitment to my podcasting journey:

_____

_____

_____

_____

DAY 2
Where Does Podcasting Fit?

Understanding where podcasting fits into:

- Your current commitments,
- Your expectations, and
- Your business goals...

is critical to its success. Because until you understand where podcasting fits, it's going to be very difficult to map out what creating and growing a podcast looks like for you.

EXERCISE:
Your Commitments, Expectations, and Business Goals

⏱ **Set a timer for 25 minutes**

When I think about my current commitments on a scale of 1–10 (1 being the lowest priority commitment I have, and 10 being the highest), podcasting gets a score of:

1   2   3   4   5   6   7   8   9   10

My expectations for my podcast could be described as:

_____

_____

_____

_____

My top 3 business SMART goals for the next 3 months are:
SMART goals are Specific, Measurable, Attainable, Relevant, and Time-bound

1. _____

2. _____

3. _____

Given my top 3 business SMART goals, my podcast fits in (write out where it fits in):

_____

_____

_____

 Recommended Resource

If you're having a tough time identifying your SMART goals right now, then a recommended resource is our Free Goals Course where we walk through step-by-step how to set and accomplish your biggest goals. Visit FreeGoalsCourse.co to get started today!

DAY 3
Your Podcast Topic, Part I of III

If you already have a topic in mind for your podcast, then this exercise will help validate it. If not, then this exercise will help you discover it.

EXERCISE:
Your Zone of Fire

⏱ **Set a timer for 30 minutes**

Using the outline below, brainstorm in the left column all the things you're passionate about—things that you love doing, and that make you happy.

In the right column, brainstorm all the things you have experience doing—things you studied in school, or that you've practiced at your previous jobs.

PASSIONS	EXPERIENCES

DAY 4
Your Podcast Topic, Part II of III

The reason you're doing this exercise over multiple days is because it's important to give yourself space between brainstorming. There might be things that come up today that you didn't even think about yesterday.

EXERCISE:
Your Zone of Fire

⏱ **Set a timer for 20 minutes**

Building on what you wrote down yesterday, continue to brainstorm your passions and experiences, and add to each of your lists.

PASSIONS | EXPERIENCES

DAY 5
Your Podcast Topic, Part III of III

Today is the day you'll either validate or create your podcast topic—this is exciting! The last couple of days have been all about what YOU believe to be your passions and experiences.

Today, it's time to find out what *others* think.

EXERCISE:
Ask Your Friends and Family

Go to 5 friends or family members and ask them this very simple question:

What do you think I'm good at?

Take note of everything your friends or family members say about what they think you're good at, and add it to your list under the appropriate column.

EXERCISE:
Identifying the Overlap

⏱ **Set a timer for 30 minutes**

Based on the list you've now been working on for 3 days, when you look at your passions and your experience, where is there overlap?

Where you find overlap = **your Zone of FIRE!**

Your Zone of FIRE is a combination of what you love doing and what you have experience doing.

There might be multiple things that overlapped for you. If so, that's great! Take some time to choose the ONE idea you'd like to pursue for your podcast topic.

My Zone of FIRE is:

_____

Now, how can you create a podcast using your Zone of FIRE that will bring value to others' lives?

My Podcast Topic is:

_____

_____

DAY 6
Proof of Concept

Now that you have a clear picture of what your podcast topic will be, it's time to get proof of concept.

EXERCISE:
Market Research

⏱ Set a timer for 10 minutes

Google your podcast topic.

Is someone else already talking about or creating content around that same or a similar idea, whether a podcast, blog, or video?

If yes, PERFECT! That's proof of concept.

Continue to look for specific examples of others who are talking about the same or similar topic on the following platforms:

- ☐ iTunes
- ☐ Amazon
- ☐ YouTube

EXERCISE:
Presentation Styles

⏱ Set a timer for 30 minutes

Once you've found someone else who is already talking about the same or a similar topic, choose your top 3 favorite sources:

1. _____

2. _____

3. _____

1. How do they present their topic?

For example, do they present in an excited, serious, or funny way? Is it long-form content that's super detailed, or do they skim the surface? Are they teaching others about that topic, or are they providing value through entertainment?

_____

_____

_____

2. What do you like about the way they present their topic?

_____

_____

_____

3. What don't you like about the way they present their topic?

_____

_____

_____

4. Given your answers to the questions above, what did you find out about the way you want to present your own topic?

_____

_____

_____

_____

5. Based on this, write how you would like to present your topic.

_____

_____

_____

_____

DAY 7
Confirm Uniqueness

Being unique is what will help you WIN with your podcast. If you're not able to stand out or stand apart from the thousands of other podcasts out there, then you will have a very tough road ahead of you.

Now that you have your podcast topic and you've researched whether someone else is already doing it (to get a better idea of how your topic is currently being—or not being—presented), it's time to confirm that YOU do it differently by adding your Unique Value Distinguisher.

Here's an example of a Unique Value Distinguisher:

Entrepreneurs On Fire was not the first podcast to interview successful entrepreneurs. But Entrepreneurs On Fire was the first podcast to do it 7 days a week. Publishing episodes daily when no one else was is an example of an Unique Value Distinguisher.

EXERCISE:
Indentifying Your Unique Value Distinguisher

 **Set a timer for 15 minutes**

1. I'm going to present my topic differently by:

_____

_____

_____

2. My Unique Value Distinguisher (UVD) is:

_____

_____

_____

3. I will add my personality to my podcast by:

_____

_____

_____

4. Other notes and ideas around how I will make my podcast unique:

_____

_____

_____

_____

_____

_____

DAY 8
Defining Your Avatar, Part I of II

Your Avatar is your ONE perfect listener for your podcast, and once you define them your podcasting journey will become a whole clearer—and easier.

Defining your avatar is so important because you'll come to 1,000 forks in the road when creating and growing your podcast. Questions like:

- What should my format be?
- How long should my episodes be?
- How often should I publish a new episode?

These should ALL be answered by your avatar, because THEY are the one you're creating your podcast for in the first place.

Because you already know what your podcast topic is going to be, defining your avatar is a natural next step.

EXERCISE:
Who Will Your Podcast Impact?

⏱ **Set a timer for 15 minutes**

Write out a description of the ONE individual who could have a life-changing experience BECAUSE they listen to your podcast:

_____

_____

_____

_____

_____

DAY 9
Defining Your Avatar, Part II of II

In yesterday's exercise you wrote out a description of the ONE individual who could have a life-changing experience BECAUSE they listen to your podcast.

Today we're going to fully define your avatar.

EXERCISE:
Getting to Know Your Avatar

⏱ **Set a timer for 30 minutes**

Review the description you created yesterday, and then watch this video about my avatar, Jimmy: EOFire.com/about.

Now let's get to know more about your avatar:

Demographics

• **Age:** _____

• **Sex:** _____

• **Marital Status:** _____

• **Education:** _____

• **Employment Status:** _____

• **Other:** _____

_____

What do they like?

_____

_____

What don't they like?

_____

_____

What are their biggest dreams and aspirations?

_____

_____

_____

What are their biggest struggles?

_____

_____

_____

WHY should they tune into your podcast?

_____

_____

_____

Based on the information you just populated, define your avatar:

_____

_____

_____

_____

_____

_____

_____

_____

_____

_____

_____

_____

DAY 10
Finding Your Avatar

Today's goal is to go out and find your avatar in real life.

EXERCISE:
Where Does Your Avatar Hang out?

⏱ Set a timer for 30 minutes

Based on your description of your avatar, where might they be hanging out?

For example, online Facebook groups, on LinkedIn, participating in online summits, attending in-person meetups, at a coffee shop, etc.

If you don't know the answer to this question, then it's time to start researching.

Go to Google, Facebook, get on the phone with a friend to brainstorm and figure out where your avatar might be hanging out.

Write down 5 specific places your avatar might hang out:

1. _____
2. _____
3. _____
4. _____
5. _____

DAY 11
Establishing a Connection with Your Avatar

Now that you have 5 places your avatar might hang out, it's time to start looking for them.

EXERCISE:
Getting to Know Your Avatar

⏱ Set a timer for 20 minutes

If this is in an online group, review the threads that have been posted. Pay attention to what different members of the group are saying in those threads (mainly, your avatar).

Write down a few of the recurring themes you've noticed during your research.

_____

_____

_____

_____

_____

If this is at an in-person meetup, what's your avatar's personality like?

_____

_____

_____

_____

_____

EXERCISE:
Establishing a Connection

Now it's time to establish a connection with your avatar.

⏱ Set a timer for 30 minutes

Introduce yourself to at least 5 people who you think are your avatar, and begin to establish a connection with them by asking questions like:

How did you find out about this group? (Based on where you found them)

_____

_____

How long have you been a part of this group?

_____

_____

What do you love most about this group?

_____

_____

What do you have going on in [a particular area of their life, ideally related to your podcast topic]?

_____

_____

If you are able to connect with any individuals whom you strongly feel are your avatar, see if they'd be willing to jump on a quick call with you.

👀 Sneak Peek

Take a sneak peek at Day 12 for a full rundown of what these calls will consist of.

DAY 12
Communicating with Your Avatar

Now that you've established a connection with at least 5 people who you think are your avatar, ask each of them if they'd be willing to jump on a 5–10–minute Skype call with you to see if a new idea you have can help them in any way.

EXERCISE:
One-On-One Calls with Your Avatar

It's okay if your one-on-one calls can't happen TODAY. The important part is that you're scheduling them. Once you've connected with your avatar for your one-on-one call, ask them questions like:

How did you get into _____ (related to your podcast topic)?

Call 1: _____

Call 2: _____

Call 3: _____

Call 4: _____

Call 5: _____

What's your biggest struggle when it comes to _____ (related to your podcast topic)?

Call 1: _____

Call 2: _____

Call 3: _____

Call 4: _____

Call 5: _____

What is it that you're looking to get out of _____ (related to your podcast topic)?

Call 1: _____

Call 2: _____

Call 3: _____

Call 4: _____

Call 5: _____

EXERCISE:
Identifying Consistencies

⏱ **Set a timer for 30 minutes**

Once your 5 calls are complete, and given the answers each individual gave you, what are some of the common themes, aspirations, and struggles you noticed while talking with these 5 different individuals?

Common themes:

_____

_____

_____

_____

_____

Common aspirations:

_____

_____

_____

_____

_____

Common struggles:

_____

_____

_____

_____

_____

Is your avatar actually who you thought they would be?
If yes, explain why. If no, what's the biggest difference?

_____

_____

_____

_____

_____

If applicable, make edits to the definition of your avatar based on what you've learned over the past couple of days.

If you don't feel you've found your avatar yet, but you know they're out there and you want to keep looking, write out a plan for how you'll go about finding and connecting with them.

_____

_____

_____

_____

_____

_____

_____

DAY 13
Your Niche

Focusing in on a niche is what will allow you to stand out. When you try and talk to everyone, you will end up talking to no one.

EXERCISE:
1 Inch Wide, 1 Mile Deep

 **Set a timer for 30 minutes**

Instead of going 1 mile wide and 1 inch deep, try going 1 inch wide and 1 mile deep.

An example of this exercise would be:

My niche is marketing for small business owners.

1 level down, my niche is Facebook marketing for small business owners.

2 levels down, my niche is Facebook marketing for small business owners who aren't currently on Facebook.

3 levels down, my niche is Facebook marketing for small business owners who aren't currently on Facebook and who have a brick-and-mortar store selling food items.

Now it's your turn...

What is your niche? (The small, specialized segment of people you're appealing to)

_____

_____

What is your niche, niched down at 1 level? (Get even more specialized)

_____

_____

_____

_____

What is your niche, niched down at 2 levels? (Get even more specialized)

_____

_____

_____

_____

What is your niche, niched down at 3 levels? (Get even more specialized)

_____

_____

_____

_____

Once you have a niche, it's going to be so much easier to go out and find exactly who you're looking to attract as a listener, and eventually, a paying customer.

DAY 14
Format, Frequency, and Length

Deciding on your format, frequency, and length will set the foundation to help you make important decisions about the setup of your podcast.

EXERCISE:
Your Podcast Format

There are several options for your podcast format. As you consider the options below, think about the type of format you'll enjoy creating the most, and what type of content your avatar will want to consume.

Check the format option that interests you most:

- ☐ Interview-based
- ☐ Topic-based
- ☐ Q&A
- ☐ Seasons/Series
- ☐ Variety show (a combination of any/all of the above)

Your format can change over time. Just make sure that any changes to your format are announced and clearly communicated to your listeners so they know what to expect.

EXERCISE:
Your Podcast Frequency and Length

When deciding on the frequency and length of your episodes, you should be considering two main factors:

1. What is possible given your current commitments?
2. What would your avatar want?

Check the frequency option you feel will be best for your podcast:

- ☐ Daily
- ☐ Twice per week
- ☐ Weekly
- ☐ Biweekly
- ☐ Monthly

If you'll be doing a season or series-based show, how often will you publish in season? How long of a break will you take in between seasons?

Check the option you feel will be best for your episode length:

- ☐ 5–10 minutes
- ☐ 15–30 minutes
- ☐ 35–60 minutes

If you're doing a variety show, then your episode length might vary based on the type of episode you're creating. Perhaps your episodes don't have a specific length—they could be as long as they need to be.

Like your format, your frequency and length can change over time, too. Just make sure that any changes to your frequency (or major changes to your length) are announced and clearly communicated to your listeners so they know what to expect.

We recommend publishing at least weekly as you start out in order to establish yourself as an authority and to gain enough momentum so that you can start growing an audience around your podcast.

Remember, consistency is KEY in podcasting, so be realistic about the frequency you can commit to, given the other things you have going on.

DAY 15
Interview and Topic-based Tips

On Day 28 you'll be heading into the creation phase of your podcast, including recording your first 3 episodes. To help you prepare for that, today we're going to focus on the setup.

EXERCISE:
Finding Guests

⏱ **Set a timer for 20 minutes**

Brainstorm where you're going to go to find potential guests for your podcast. Some recommendations include:

- ☐ Looking at speaker lineups for top conferences in your industry or niche
- ☐ Using services like Interview Valet
- ☐ Connecting and building relationships with others in your industry or niche via social media (Facebook, Twitter, LinkedIn, Instagram)
- ☐ Asking guests you have on your show to recommend one person they think would be a good fit

I will find potential guests for my podcast by doing the following:

1. _____
2. _____
3. _____
4. _____
5. _____

EXERCISE:
Booking Guests

⏱ Set a timer for 30 minutes

You can book guests for your podcast most efficiently by using scheduling software to help.

Research the following scheduling software options and choose the one you'll use to help you streamline scheduling guests on your show:

- ☐ ScheduleOnce (recommended)
- ☐ Calendly
- ☐ Acuity Scheduling

I will use _____ to help me book guests on my show.

EXERCISE:
Interview Checklist

⏱ Set a timer for 15 minutes

Make sure you have an interview checklist you can use every time you connect with a guest to record an interview, so you don't miss any important steps.

- You can check out a sample interview checklist here: EOFire.com/interviewchecklist.

Write out a draft of your interview checklist here:

_____

_____

_____

_____

_____

_____

EXERCISE:
Finding Topics

⏱ **Set a timer for 15 minutes**

Brainstorm ways you're going to come up with topics for your show. Some recommendations include:

- ☐ Search for trending content on social media and big name sites in your industry/niche
- ☐ Make note of ideas that resonate with you when reading books or others' blogs
- ☐ Ask your avatar (whom you've connected with already) what topics they'd like to hear about
- ☐ Set up Google Alerts for your keywords to see what other top sites are writing about

Write out a draft strategy you can use for finding topics for your show:

_____

_____

_____

EXERCISE:
Start Your Topic List

🕐 **Set a timer for 20 minutes**

Start a topics list using your favorite note-taking software. Some recommendations include:

- ☐ Workflowy
- ☐ Google Drive
- ☐ Evernote
- ☐ Pen & paper

Once you've chosen your note-taking software, add at least 5 topic ideas to your list. You can also include them here:

_____

_____

_____

_____

_____

DAY 16
Initial Keyword Research

Doing initial keyword research for your podcast is mandatory if you want to be able to rank and be found by your avatar.

EXERCISE:
Finding Your Keywords

⏱ Set a timer for 30 minutes

Start your initial research using the Google AdWords keyword planner and by searching iTunes.

What would your avatar type into a search if they were looking for your podcast?

☐ _____

☐ _____

☐ _____

What comes up in Google keyword planner when you type these words into the search volume data and trends?

☐ Average monthly searches _____

☐ Competition _____

☐ Average monthly searches _____

☐ Competition _____

What comes up in iTunes when you type these words into the search?

☐ _____

☐ _____

☐ _____

After your initial research, what are your top 3 keywords you want to rank for?

1. _____

2. _____

3. _____

Keep these keywords in mind for naming your podcast—and later, for descriptions and episode titles.

DAY 17
Naming Your Podcast

You know your podcast topic, you've defined your avatar, you've identified your niche, and you have a pretty good idea of what some of your strongest keywords will be.

Now is a perfect time to come up with a name that will help represent everything your listeners will get when they tune into your podcast.

EXERCISE:
Brainstorming Your Podcast Name

 Set a timer for 30 minutes

Brainstorm several different names for your podcast, keeping in mind that your podcast name should ALWAYS be CLEAR FIRST, clever second (and only if it's a value add).

Also, remember to think about your avatar when naming your podcast. Your podcast name should SPEAK DIRECTLY TO your avatar, and when they see it they should immediately know:

1. That your podcast IS for them
2. Exactly what they're going to get when they tune in

Finally, you want to consider length and keywords when naming your podcast. The strongest podcast names are straight to the point and include at least 1 of your main keywords.

You can include anything you're not able to include in your podcast name that you think is important for your listeners to know about your podcast in your tagline.

5 Podcast names I like:

1. _____
2. _____
3. _____
4. _____
5. _____

5 Podcast taglines I like:

1. _____
2. _____
3. _____
4. _____
5. _____

Put each name and tagline through the check:

- ☐ Is the URL available?
- ☐ Search iTunes and Google: is someone else already using it?
- ☐ Clear first, clever second (and only if it's a value add)
- ☐ Speaks directly to your avatar
- ☐ At least 1 keyword is present (bonus)

Once you decide on your podcast name, you should:

- ☐ Purchase the domain using a service like GoDaddy or BlueHost
- ☐ Create social media profiles with the name (Facebook, Twitter, Instagram, etc.)

DAY 18
Legal Considerations for Your Podcast

As you're creating your podcast it's important to be aware of legal considerations. We are not lawyers, nor should you consider this section legal advice. If you're concerned about legal-related matters, then you should reach out to a lawyer who can help guide you.

 Recommended Resource

LegalZoom.com is a great place to start. You can also reach out to our lawyer, David Lizerbram, and he can point you in the right direction: LizerbramLaw.com/contact.

EXERCISE:
Do Your Due Diligence

 Set a timer for 30 minutes

If you've already found out someone else is using the podcast name you're dead-set on, then do some research to find out:

- ☐ Is it in the same industry/niche as you?
- ☐ How active is it?
- ☐ Do they have a business built around it?

if you've found someone else is already actively using the podcast name you want to use, then consider contacting someone for legal advice.

If you plan to monetize your podcast, then you should consider what type of entity to establish (sole proprietor, LLC, etc.)

💡 Recommended Resource

Find out what business entity is right for you. Visit CPAOnFire.com/firenation for your free course!

As you start to develop and produce your podcast, make sure you're using music, references, and other audio clips that are royalty-free. A great site for this is AudioJungle.net.

The
IDEA PHASE
REVIEW

"Have patience with all things, But, first of all with yourself."

— Saint Francis de Sales

DAY 19
Idea Phase Review

CONGRATULATIONS! Over the past 18 days you've made A LOT of progress towards launching your own podcast!

Let's review:

My WHY for my podcast is:

_____

_____

My declaration that I'm fully committed to my podcasting journey:

_____

_____

My Podcast topic is:

_____

My Unique Value Distinguisher is:

_____

My Avatar is:

_____

_____

_____

_____

My Niche is:

_____

The format, frequency, and length of my podcast will be:

Format: _____

Frequency: _____

Length: _____

The name of my Podcast is:

_____

Other notes and reflection from The Idea Phase:

_____

_____

_____

_____

_____

_____

_____

_____

_____

_____

_____

The
SETUP PHASE

"You don't make progress by standing on the sidelines, whimpering and complaining. You make progress by implementing ideas."

— Shirley Chisholm

DAY 20
Recommended Equipment

Deciding on what equipment you'll use for podcasting doesn't have to be a scary or overwhelming process. It doesn't have to cost a lot of money either.

The simplest way to get started is to have 3 main pieces of equipment —all necessary to create a great-sounding podcast:

- Your computer
- Your microphone
- Your headphones

There are loads of gadgets and upgrades beyond these 3 pieces of equipment you can leverage for your podcast, but until you've launched, built a strong foundation for your podcast, and have started growing an audience, this is a perfect place to start.

Our top recommendations for the equipment absolutely required to create a great-sounding podcast:

- MacBook Pro laptop or Mac desktop
- Audio-Technica ATR2100 Microphone
- Apple earbuds

For on-the-go/portable recording

- Option 1: Zoom H4N portable handheld recorder with built-in microphones
- Option 2: Your mobile device with lapel microphone

Recommended Resource

We've put together a complete—and always-up-to-date—list of our recommended equipment for you here: EOFire.com/equipment.

This includes the accessories and links for everything we use here at Entrepreneurs On Fire.

EXERCISE:
Choosing Your Podcast Equipment

Once you've reviewed our recommended resources and done your own research, it's time to choose your podcast equipment.

Set a timer for 15 minutes

The podcast equipment I will use:

☐ Computer: _____

☐ Microphone: _____

☐ Headphones: _____

DAY 21
Recommended Software

The podcast software you use is going to heavily depend on your equipment setup—mainly which computer you're using: Mac or PC.

If you're using a Mac, here is our recommended software setup:

To connect with guests and record interviews

- Option 1: Skype and Ecamm call recorder
- Option 2: Zencastr

To record solo shows and/or to edit your podcast episodes

- Option 1: Adobe Audition
- Option 2: GarageBand (free)

If you're using a PC, here is our recommended software setup:

To connect with guests and record interviews

- Option 1: Zencastr
- Option 2: RINGR

To record solo shows and/or to edit your podcast episodes

- Option 1: Adobe Audition
- Option 2: Audacity (free)

For Video Podcasting

- Option 1: Zoom.us
- Option 2: YouTube Live

Note: If you will be doing a solo, topic-based podcast then you can record directly into your software.

 Recommended Resource

We've put together a complete—and always-up-to-date—list of our recommended software for you here: EOFire.com/equipment.

This includes the accessories and links for everything we use here at Entrepreneurs On Fire.

EXERCISE:
Choosing Your Podcast Software

Once you've reviewed our recommended resources and done your own research, it's time to choose your podcast software.

⏱ Set a timer for 15 minutes

The podcast software I will use:

☐ For my recording setup: _____

☐ For my editing: _____

DAY 22
Set Up Your Template and Keyboard Shortcuts

Regardless of the software you've chosen to record and edit your podcast, you have the option to create a template.

Creating a template prevents you from having to re-enter your settings every time you go to record and/or edit an episode, and the settings you choose will have a big impact on your audio quality.

For example, having a Hard Limiter set in your template will help you bring all bits up to a certain level, without any specific bits coming across louder than the others.

Today it's your goal to set up your template.

EXERCISE:
Set up Your Template

Whether you're using Adobe Audition, Audacity, or GarageBand, there is a video tutorial waiting for you here: EOFire.com/template.

⏱ **Set a timer for 20 minutes**

Notes for setting up your template:

_____

_____

_____

_____

_____

_____

_____

_____

Once your template is set up, it's time to set up your keyboard shortcuts for editing. This will save you massive amounts of time and make it easy to edit your podcast episodes.

EXERCISE:
Set up Your Keyboard Shortcuts

Whether you're using Adobe Audition, Audacity, or Garageband, there is a video tutorial waiting for you here: EOFire.com/shortcuts.

⏱ **Set a timer for 20 minutes**

I will set up keyboard shortcuts for the following functions:

☐ **Insert Silence (example)**

☐ _____

☐ _____

☐ _____

☐ _____

☐ _____

☐ _____

DAY 23
Sample Recording and Editing Part I of II

Now that you have your equipment, software, your template, and your keyboard shortcuts set up, it's time to dive into recording and editing!

Today, you're going to record your first practice episode.

It doesn't have to be long or perfect—in fact, it won't be. The point is to start becoming familiar with your software and the settings you've chosen.

For a video that will help you with your first recording and editing session, visit EOFire.com/practice.

👓 Sneak Peek

Take a sneak peek at Day 24. Tomorrow you'll be doing another sample recording, only it will be with a guest! Think of a friend, family member, or accountability partner you can reach out to and ask to do a practice interview with you.

EXERCISE:
Sample Recording

⏱ Set a timer for 30 minutes

As you're getting set up and recording your practice episode, make note of the specific steps you're taking.

(For example, open Adobe Audition, check my microphone settings, make sure my earbuds are plugged in, test my audio quality, etc.)

Step 1: _____

Step 2: _____

Step 3: _____

Step 4: _____

Step 5: _____

Now hit record!

Once you've recorded your practice episode, play it back and just listen. Then, fill in the blanks below:

I want to improve upon:
(For example, saying "umm" or using a particular "filler word" too often)

_____

_____

_____

_____

The things I liked about my practice episode are:
(For example, my personality, energy, transitions, etc.)

_____

_____

_____

_____

EXERCISE:
Editing Your Sample Recording

⏱ Set a timer for 20 minutes

Now it's time to practice editing.

Play your episode back again, and this time, practice making edits.

Once you're finished with your practice recording and editing session, make note of the things that stood out to you. This might be things that you didn't expect, things you really enjoyed, or things you need to practice more.

Things I didn't expect:

_____

_____

_____

_____

Things I really enjoyed:

_____

_____

_____

_____

Things I need to practice:

_____

_____

_____

_____

DAY 24
Sample Recording and Editing Part II of II

Today, you're going to mirror what you did yesterday, only you're going to do it with another person!

Ask a friend, family member, or accountability partner to do a practice interview with you. Again, the point is not to have this be perfectly planned out and executed. The point is that you're getting on the mic and practicing.

EXERCISE:
Sample Recording

⏱ **Set a timer for 30 minutes**

As you're getting set up and recording your interview episode, make note of the specific steps you're taking.

(For example, open Adobe Audition, check my microphone settings, make sure my earbuds are plugged in, test my audio quality, open Skype and connect with my interviewee, have a pre-interview chat, etc.)

Step 1: _____

Step 2: _____

Step 3: _____

Step 4: _____

Step 5: _____

Step 6: _____

Now hit record!

Once you've recorded your practice interview episode, thank your guest for recording with you, and then play it back and just listen. Then, fill in the blanks below:

I want to improve upon:
(For example, saying "umm" or using a particular "filler word" too often)

_____

_____

_____

_____

The things I liked about my practice interview are:
(For example, my personality, energy, transitions, etc.)

_____

_____

_____

_____

EXERCISE:
Editing your sample recording

⏱ Set a timer for 20 minutes

Now it's time to practice editing.

Play your episode back again, and this time, practice making edits.

Once you're finished with your practice interview recording and editing session, make note of the things that stood out to you.

This might be things that you didn't expect, things you really enjoyed, or things you need to practice more.

Things I didn't expect:

_____
_____
_____
_____

Things I really enjoyed:

_____
_____
_____
_____

Things I need to practice:

_____
_____
_____
_____

👀 Sneak Peek

Take a sneak peek at Day 35. This is when you'll be recording your first 2 episodes. If you will be doing a topic-based show, start thinking about the topics you'll discuss in your first 2 episodes.

If you'll be doing an interview-based show, now would be a good time to request at least 5 guests on your show, with the recording date being Day 35.

Topics to discuss in first 2 episodes:

1. _____
2. _____

Potential guests to interview in first 2 episodes:

1. _____
2. _____
3. _____
4. _____
5. _____

 **Recommended Resource**

Check out the sample email templates for requesting a guest on your show at EOFire.com/guestemail.

DAY 25
Exporting and Tagging Your MP3

After you record and edit your episodes it's time to export and tag your MP3 file. Today we're going to practice doing just that.

EXERCISE:
Exporting and Tagging Your MP3

⏱ Set a timer for 20 minutes

Follow the instructions for exporting your MP3 file based on the recording and editing software you're using found here: EOFire.com/export.

Once you've exported your MP3 file, download the ID3 Editor here: pa-software.com/id3editor.

Follow this video tutorial for instructions on how to tag your MP3 file using ID3 Editor: EOFire.com/id3.

Tagging your MP3 file is important because it attaches metadata to your episode that helps iTunes and other platforms organize it in rankings. So including things like your show name, the title of your episode, and the keywords you want to rank for is important.

DAY 26
Your Media Host

Your media host is where you'll upload your podcast episodes to be syndicated on the different platforms, like iTunes, Stitcher Radio, and Google Play.

Our top recommendation for your podcast media host is Podcast Websites.

Podcast Websites is your all-in-one podcast and website hosting solution, and it's a software platform we've teamed up with Mark Asquith to create.

You can choose to only host your podcast with Podcast Websites, or you can host your podcast AND your website on the platform.

To learn more about Podcast Websites, visit PodcastWebsites.com.

EXERCISE:
Choose Your Media Host

⏱ **Set a timer for 15 minutes**

Spend some time checking out your podcast media host options; there are several of them out there, and you need to find the one that's right for you.

Podcast Websites is an all-in-one website and podcast hosting solution. So if you're just starting out and are looking for a website platform built specifically by podcasters, for podcasters that comes with 24/7 support and a drag-and-drop builder for your website, then this is the way to go.

My media host is:

_____

The
SETUP PHASE
REVIEW

"All great achievements require time."

— Maya Angelou

DAY 27
The Setup Phase Review

This past week has been JAM PACKED with some incredible action! You've got to feel GREAT about the progress you're making—congratulations!

Let's review the things you've completed over the past week...

The equipment I chose:

☐ **Computer:** _____

☐ **Microphone:** _____

☐ **Headphones:** _____

The software I chose:

☐ **To record:** _____

☐ **To edit:** _____

My biggest lesson learned from recording and editing my practice solo episode:

_____

_____

_____

My biggest lesson learned from recording and editing my practice interview episode:

_____

_____

_____

My media host is:

_____

Other notes and reflection from the past 7 days:

_____

_____

_____

_____

_____

_____

_____

_____

_____

_____

The
CREATION PHASE

"I've missed more than 9,000 shots in my career. I've lost almost 300 games. 26 times I've been trusted to take the game's winning shot and missed. I've failed over and over and over again in my life and that's why I succeed."

— Michael Jordan

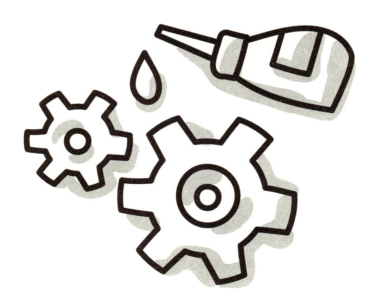

DAY 28
Your Podcast Mission Statement

Your podcast mission statement clearly communicates your core values, along with the WHY and purpose of your podcast.

Having a mission statement you can refer to in order to ground yourself and that you can share with others (including potential guests if you're doing an interview-based show) will be key.

EXERCISE:
Write Your Podcast Mission Statement

⏱ **Set a timer for 20 minutes**

My Podcast Mission Statement:

_____

_____

_____

_____

_____

_____

_____

_____

_____

_____

_____

_____

_____

_____

DAY 29
Your Podcast Artwork

Your podcast artwork is a visual representation of what your podcast is all about.

While your podcast artwork is very important, it can be changed, so it shouldn't hold you back from launching your show.

Your podcast artwork, like your podcast name, should be straightforward and clearly communicate to your avatar what they're going to get when they tune in.

There are podcast artwork specifications that you must follow for iTunes. Visit EOFire.com/artwork to confirm the current iTunes artwork specifications.

EXERCISE:
Creating Your Artwork

⏱ Set a timer for 30 minutes

Start brainstorming ideas for your podcast artwork. As you begin, be sure to consider the following:

- ☐ Not too crowded or busy
- ☐ Text is big and easy to read (it's going to be very small in the iTunes store)
- ☐ Clearly communicates what your podcast is about

Now like me, you may not be a designer, and so you might be wondering where you can go to get a great looking logo. But this will depend on your budget and how "DIY" you're willing to get.

If you want to design your own logo, some great options are:

- ☐ Canva.com
- ☐ PicMonkey.com
- ☐ Photoshop (if you know design)

If you want to have someone else design your logo, some great options are:

- ☐ Fiverr.com
- ☐ DesignCrowd.com/fire (special savings await!)

Here are some brainstorming ideas to help you get started with what you want your podcast logo to look like.

If you are going to hire a designer, share this information with them to help them get an idea of what you're looking for.

I want the look and feel of my logo to be:

_____

The colors I want to use in my logo are:

_____

The icon that I think best represents my topic and/or industry is:

_____

Things I definitely do not want in my logo are:

_____

_____

The font(s) I would like to use:

_____

Other notes about my logo:

_____

_____

_____

_____

If you're having a hard time describing how you want your artwork to look and feel visit the Podcast Store in iTunes for examples.

DAY 30
Your Episode Flow

For interview-based podcasts, your flow will consist of the questions you're going to ask your interviewees and the different phases of each episode.

For topic-based podcasts, the flow will be the outline each of your episodes follow. For example:

- An intro
- A lesson
- A reflection on that lesson
- A wrap-up

No matter which format you chose for your show, putting together a flow will help you create a system around your content creation, which will be instrumental in helping you create valuable content on a consistent basis moving forward.

EXERCISE:
Create Your Episode Flow

⏱ **Set a timer for 30 minutes**

Check out some examples of different episode flows based on the type of podcast you're creating here: EOFire.com/sampleflow.

Based on the format of your show, what will your episode flow be?

My episode flow:

_____
_____
_____
_____
_____
_____
_____
_____
_____
_____
_____
_____
_____
_____
_____
_____

DAY 31
Your Podcast Scheduler

We recommend always scheduling one month ahead of your show.

In order to create this much content—the exact number of episodes will depend on the frequency of your show—you need to have a system in place that you can use now and moving forward.

Batching your recording for maximum efficiency is the best way to go. For example, record 4 interviews in 1 day versus 4 interviews on 4 different days.

How many interviews or episodes you can record in a row might be less now than in a few months from now (once you've gotten used to your process). That's okay; just continue practicing and never compromise quality.

EXERCISE:
Create Your Schedule

 Set a timer for 45 minutes

To start...

Interview-based shows
(*example based on a weekly podcast*)

- Come up with a list of 20 people you want to interview (reference Day 15 for how)
- Start reaching out to them now and request to have them on your show
- Using your scheduler, book at least 6 weeks worth of interviews (that's 6 yeses out of 20)

Given this example, you'll have 6 weeks worth of content once you're finished recording.

When creating your schedule be sure to consider how long it's going to take you to record, edit, and upload.

Also remember that you control the schedule. If you're looking to book 6 guests, open up 4 time slots next Tuesday, and 4 times next Friday.

That gives your 6 guests 8 potential time slots and you only 2 recording days.

Once you create your schedule, stick with it! While you'll be 6 weeks ahead once you complete the cycle above, the clock is always ticking. You should have a schedule in place that allows you to always be adding to your content bank on a consistent basis, so that you're always at least 4–6 weeks ahead at any given time.

Topic-based shows
(*example based on a weekly podcast*)

- Come up with a list of 20 topics you want to cover (reference Day 15 for how)
- Create an episode outline for at least 6 of those topics
- Schedule time on your calendar to record those 6 episodes

Given this example, you'll have 6 weeks worth of content once you're finished recording.

The most critical step in your plan is the last one: consistently scheduling the time in your calendar to sit down and record, edit, and upload your episodes.

Podcasting is a marathon, not a sprint. Each time you schedule a recording day, push yourself to find out what your max recording number is and start to craft your schedule around that.

Remember, your schedule has to be recurring and consistent. While you'll be 6 weeks ahead once you complete the cycle above, the clock is always ticking.

My podcast schedule:

_____
_____
_____
_____
_____
_____
_____
_____
_____
_____
_____
_____
_____
_____
_____

DAY 32
Your Content's Goal

Making sure your content has a goal every time helps ensure:

1. You're not just creating content for the sake of creating content;
2. You actually have a plan in place to maximize your content

Each piece of content you create might have a different goal. For example, the goal of one episode might be to help grow your email list, while the goal of another episode might be to engage with your listeners one-on-one.

EXERCISE:
Brainstorming Content Goals

 **Set a timer for 15 minutes**

Become familiar with the questions below. You should be asking yourself these questions (or ones that you come up with on your own) every time you create a new episode.

I believe this episode will be valuable for my listeners because:

_____
_____
_____

I have a clear message or lesson to deliver in this episode, which is:

_____
_____
_____

The goal of this episode is to:

_____

_____

_____

I'm going to accomplish this goal by: (what Call to Action will you use?)

_____

_____

_____

Once my listeners take this action, the next step that will happen is: (what happens once they do what you told them to do?)

_____

_____

_____

DAY 33
Your Podcast Intro and Outro

There are two options for creating your podcast intro and outro:

1. Hire someone to create it for you;
2. Create it yourself.

There are pros and cons to each:

1. Hire someone to create it for you

- Pro: It helps build credibility—especially when you're first starting out—to have a professionally recorded intro/outro
- Con: It can be a little pricey, depending on where you go to get it done

2. Create it yourself

- Pro: You can save some money and get creative with it—plus it'll be consistent with your energy and voice.
- Con: You'll be losing out on the added credibility

Whether you decide to hire someone or create it yourself, remember: you can always change it!

 Recommended Resource

For our top recommended resources for hiring or for creating your intro and outro visit: EOFire.com/podcastintro.

DAY 34
Recording Episode 000

One of your most important episodes is Episode 000. This is your intro episode and is oftentimes the most listened-to episode on any podcast.

The reason being: if someone new finds your podcast and wants to know whether it's for them, they'll look for the very first episode where the host introduces the show and what listeners can expect.

So Episode 000 is just that: your introductory episode where you not only let your listeners know a little about you and why you're doing the podcast, but also what they can expect if they continue to tune in.

👀 Sneak Peek

Take a sneak peak at Day 36. Today you'll record Episode 000, and on Day 36 you'll be editing it.

Pro tip: When recording your episodes, if you mess up or want to correct something, do a 2-second pause. This way, when you look back at your WAV file, you'll be able to quickly spot the areas you know you need to edit.

EXERCISE:
Creating Episode 000

⏱ Set a timer for 30 minutes

Episode 000 typically runs between 5–10 minutes. Here's a loose outline you can follow, but remember, this is YOUR podcast—be unique!

Episode 000 Outline

About me (estimated time: 2–3 minutes)

- Introduce yourself—people build relationships with people, so tell your audience a bit about your background
- Why did you decide to start the podcast? Share your excitement with your audience!

_____

_____

_____

_____

_____

What your podcast will be about (estimated time: 3–4 minutes)

- "What's in it for me—the listener?"
- Share the vision and direction of your podcast so your listeners know whether or not it's for them
- Ask for feedback! Ask your audience for engagement and let them know up front that you welcome it

_____

_____

_____

_____

_____

_____

_____

_____

_____

Frequency (estimated time: 1-2 minutes)

- Episode 000 is your opportunity to explain what the frequency is going to be and anything that might be different about your "launch period" (For example, I'm launching with 3 episodes, then I plan to go to 2x per week, or whatever that may be...)

_____

_____

_____

EXERCISE:
Record Episode 000

 Set a timer for 15 minutes

Should you update Episode 000 at any point?

Sure! You can update it any time! If you change the format, frequency, or direction of your show, or after several months find that your show has taken on a new tone, update Episode 000 so those tuning in know that you've changed it up.

It's also a good idea to create an update episode in real time if you make major changes to your show—like format, frequency, etc., so your current listeners know what to expect.

If you haven't recorded Episode 000 yet, but launched another podcast a long time ago, it's not too late to record and add it now. Just backdate it so that it shows up as the first episode in your feed!

Now it's time to hit record!

Editing notes:

_____

_____

_____

_____

_____

_____

DAY 35
Recording Your First 2 Episodes

We recommend launching your podcast with 3 episodes, which we'll be going into detail about in the launch strategy section.

For right now, let's focus on recording your first 2 "regular" episodes.

Based on the format, frequency, length, and flow of your podcast, record your first 2 episodes using the outline below to help guide you.

👀 Sneak Peek

Take a sneak peek at Day 36. Today you'll record your first 2 episodes, and tomorrow you'll be editing and adding your intro and outro.

Pro tip: When recording your episodes, if you mess up or want to correct something, do a 2-second pause. This way, when you look back at your WAV file, you'll be able to quickly spot the areas you know you need to edit.

EPISODE 1

Title: _____

Description:

_____

_____

_____

Flow:

_____

_____

_____

_____

My episode checklist (so you don't forget any steps!)

1. _____
2. _____
3. _____
4. _____
5. _____

My content outline

1. _____
2. _____
3. _____
4. _____
5. _____

☐ Hit record!

To-do's after recording:

1. _____
2. _____
3. _____
4. _____
5. _____

Editing notes:

_____
_____
_____
_____
_____
_____

EPISODE 2

Title: _____

Description:

_____

_____

_____

Flow:

_____

_____

_____

_____

My episode checklist (so you don't forget any steps!)

1. _____
2. _____
3. _____
4. _____
5. _____

My content outline

1. _____
2. _____
3. _____
4. _____
5. _____

☐ Hit record!

To-do's after recording:

1. _____
2. _____
3. _____
4. _____
5. _____

Editing notes:

_____
_____
_____
_____
_____
_____

DAY 36
Editing Your Episodes

On Day 22 you set up your template and keyboard shortcuts in your recording and editing software, and today you'll reap the benefits of having that template and those keyboard shortcuts set up!

EXERCISE:
Edit Your Episodes

⏱ Set a timer for 45 minutes

It's time to edit Episode 000 and your first 2 episodes!

Before you dive in, take a look back at Day 33 and remember, part of the editing process is pulling in your intro and outro.

Also take a look back at Day 34 and Day 35, and review your editing notes to refresh your memory.

Now, it's time to dive into editing your first 3 episodes!

As you're editing, use the section below to take any notes you think might help you improve your editing process moving forward.

☐ Start editing!

Ways I could improve my editing process:

_____

_____

_____

_____

_____

_____

The
CREATION PHASE REVIEW

"Ideas are easy. Implementation is hard."

— *Guy Kawasaki*

DAY 37
The Creation Phase Review

We've covered loads of greatness over the past 9 days. Let's review everything you've accomplished!

My Podcast Mission Statement:

_____

_____

_____

_____

_____

_____

☐ My Podcast Artwork is in the works!

My episode flow:

_____

_____

_____

_____

_____

_____

_____

_____

_____

_____

_____

_____

_____

☐ My Podcast Schedule is in place!

☐ I have my content goal and questions set

☐ I've created my intro and outro (or have hired someone else to create it for me)

My biggest lesson learned from recording Episode 000 plus my first 2 episodes is:

_____

_____

_____

My biggest lesson learned from editing my first 3 episodes is:

_____

_____

_____

The
PRE-LAUNCH PHASE

*"If you're not embarrassed by the first version of your product,
you've launched too late. "*

-— Reid Hoffman

DAY 38
Your Launch Strategy

Today we're going to review 3 strategies to help you crush your launch!

1. Launching with 3 episodes

We recommend launching your podcast with 3 episodes:

- Episode 000
- 2 regular episodes

This is so that when people find your podcast when you've first launched they know exactly what to expect from your Episode 000 and they have a good taste of what's to come without having to wait for your next publish date.

This also will help you get an initial push for momentum. As far as we know, iTunes bases their rankings at least partially on downloads within the last 24 hours. That being the case, launching with 3 episodes gives you 3x the downloads.

We caution against launching with more than 3 episodes though, because if you launch with 10 episodes and have 10x the downloads, but then go for a week without any additional downloads, the difference could do the opposite to your ranking.

2. Your launch team

On Day 42 we're going to focus on your launch team, but know that this could play a big role in your launch strategy.

The idea is that you'll get a group of friends, family members, and/or colleagues together to help you spread the word about your new podcast leading up to and on the day it launches.

When building out a launch team you want to find those who are ready and willing to commit to supporting you, and those who understand and can clearly communicate your mission.

Your launch team request could be as simple as "please share my podcast with your friends, family, and followers the day it goes live," or it could be as in-depth as "here's a checklist of the 8 things I'm asking you to do the week of my launch."

3. Communications plan

Your launch team aside, you should also have your own communications plan in place.

This might include:

- A press release about your upcoming podcast (if relevant),
- Guest blog posts on other's sites in your industry or niche,
- Guest podcast appearances on other podcasts in your industry or niche,
- Social media announcements, and
- Any type of emails or announcements you're able to send to your own contacts.

The most important part about your communications plan is that it's working together to help you build momentum and be in as many different places at once as possible.

EXERCISE:
Your Launch Plan Outline

⏱ **Set a timer for 30 minutes**

1. If you haven't already completed your intro episode plus 2 more for your launch, revisit Day 34, 35, and 36 to complete them.

☐ Episode 000 complete!

☐ My first 2 episodes are complete!

2. Brainstorm at least 10 people you can ask to be a part of your launch team and reach out to them with your ask.

1. _____   6. _____
2. _____   7. _____
3. _____   8. _____
4. _____   9. _____
5. _____   10. _____

3. Create a plan you can execute for your communications, with specific steps and deadlines to hold yourself accountable.

Deliverable   Due Date

_____   _____
_____   _____
_____   _____
_____   _____
_____   _____
_____   _____
_____   _____
_____   _____
_____   _____

DAY 39
Setting Goals for Launch

It's important that you set goals up front for your launch and beyond so you know whether you're hitting the mark. As you approach launch day, think about what a GREAT launch would look like for you.

Your goals are what YOU would consider a win, not what other people say you should be doing.

EXERCISE:
A GREAT Launch

⏱ **Set a timer for 10 minutes**

Brainstorm what a GREAT launch would look like for you:

An example might be:

The day I launch my podcast I will celebrate with family and friends this great accomplishment I've worked SO hard to get to, and within 1 week of my launch I will have 100 downloads and will have connected with at least 1 listener of my podcast via social media, email, or from the contact form on my website.

My Launch Goal is:

_____

_____

_____

_____

EXERCISE:
Setting Ongoing Goals for Your Podcast

🕐 **Set a timer for 30 minutes**

Repeat the same exercise for your 1-month, 3-month, and 6-month goals.

My 1-month Goal is:

_____

_____

_____

_____

My 3-month Goal is:

_____

_____

_____

_____

My 6-month Goal is:

_____

_____

_____

_____

DAY 40
Your Podcast Website

As you approach launch day you should be thinking about your home base: your website.

If you already have a website for an existing business, and your podcast is going to be a part of that business, it's a great idea to add your podcast to your existing site.

If you don't already have a website, then it's a good idea to get one in place so your listeners have a place to go to get in touch with you and find out more about you and what you have to offer.

A great platform, and one that we co-own, is called Podcast Websites.

We created Podcast Websites to be your all-in-one podcast website and hosting solution, because when we started, nothing like it existed. In fact, there still isn't anything out there like it, because we include everything you need to host your website and podcast under 1 roof— including 24/7 support.

Plus, Podcast Websites is built on Wordpress, so anything you can do on Wordpress you can do on Podcast Websites.

EXERCISE:
Your Podcast Website

 Set a timer for 15 minutes

If you don't already have a website:

Research and confirm the platform you'll use for your website.

My website will be on:

Once your website is ready for setup (or if you already have a website), here's a checklist of 3 things every podcast website needs.

3 Things Every Website Needs

- ☐ Home page with a giveaway and email opt in
- ☐ Podcast tab where people can listen to your podcast
- ☐ Contact page where people can get in touch with you

DAY 41
Social Media Presence

Today we're going to focus on your social media presence, and we're going to start with one single platform.

Unlike what most people say about "being everywhere" on social media, we believe you should only be in the places that make sense— for example, where your avatar is.

So if your avatar isn't on Instagram, then don't worry about Instagram. Likewise, if they aren't on LinkedIn, then no need to worry about LinkedIn.

EXERCISE:
Choosing Your Social Focus

 **Set a timer for 30 minutes**

So let's start with ONE social platform where you know your avatar is hanging out.

My ONE platform is: _____

Once you have your ONE platform, start to build out a system so you can begin (or continue) building a presence on that channel as:

- A leader
- An authority
- A credible source
- A valuable person to follow

This will include making sure:

- You're consistent
- You have value to share (not just your own content)
- You have a social media scheduler in place
- You set aside time to engage

To start, you're simply going to build a bank of content you can share on your ONE platform. This will include a mix of all different kinds of things depending on what your audience will find valuable.

It might be a mix of:

- Other leaders' content in your industry or niche
- Your insights around hot topics
- Inspirational quotes/images
- A glance into your personal life
- Your own content

The golden rule here is to always lead with value.

Choose your social media scheduler. Some options include:

☐ Hootsuite

☐ dlvr.it

☐ Meet Edgar

Once you've chosen the scheduler you'll use, spend the rest of your time populating it with social content scheduled to go out over the next week. Gaining momentum on social media through posting valuable content before you launch your podcast is a great strategy. This way, once you do launch your podcast, you'll already have people following you.

Depending on the channel you're using, you might schedule 1-2 posts per day (Instagram, Facebook, LinkedIn) or 5-6 posts per day (Twitter, Pinterest).

DAY 42
Your Launch Team

We touched on building your launch team on Day 38, but now we're going to break down what this will actually look like once they say yes.

First, you want to make sure you're supporting your launch team and getting them the information, assets, and anything else they need to successfully spread the word about your podcast.

An example might be putting together a password-protected page on your website that only they have access to.

On this page you could include sample social media posts, graphics they can use, and any other info relevant to what you're asking them to do. This will be a central place everyone can go to find exactly what they need.

Make it easy for them to help support you!

EXERCISE:
Your Launch Team Assets

 **Set a timer for 30 minutes**

Create an outline of the page you'll share with your launch team. Once your outline is complete, start creating the assets you'll need and upload/link them on the page.

Be sure to reach out to your launch team and share this info with them!

DAY 43
Spreading the Word

Spreading the word about your podcast doesn't happen overnight; it needs to happen consistently over time in order to build momentum and start to stick.

Plus, this is an exciting time for you! You should be FIRED UP to get the word out about what it is you're creating. After all, that's how you make a big impact!

EXERCISE:
Podcast Awareness Template

⏱ **Set a timer for 30 minutes**

To help you spread the word about your podcast, here are some ideas of things you could put together. Choose at least 3 and create them now.

- ☐ An email template that explains the purpose of your podcast and why people would want to listen
- ☐ Social media copy you can recycle that shares your excitement for your upcoming podcast (and why people who follow you should care)
- ☐ A giveaway or contest to get others excited about being involved in your launch (be sure you're checking on giveaway and contest rules before engaging)
- ☐ A fun audio or video clip you can share with people
- ☐ Business cards that help people find your website and podcast
- ☐ Flyers that you could take to local spots where you know your avatar is hanging out

☐ Attend any local meetups or gatherings as often as possible to meet those who could become fans of your podcast and content

Notes for how I will spread the word about my podcast:

_____

_____

_____

_____

_____

_____

_____

_____

_____

_____

_____

_____

_____

_____

_____

_____

_____

_____

_____

_____

_____

_____

_____

_____

_____

_____

The
PRE-LAUNCH PHASE REVIEW

"Every great dream begins with a dreamer. Always remember, you have within you the strength, the patience, and the passion to reach for the stars to change the world. "

— Harriet Tubman

DAY 44
The Pre-Launch Phase Review

You should be very proud of the progress you've made up to this point—you're SO CLOSE to launching your podcast!

☐ I have my launch strategy set

My Podcast launch goal is:

_____

_____

_____

_____

☐ My Podcast Website is set up and I have the 3 things every website needs.

My ONE Social Media platform is: _____

☐ I have populated content in my social media scheduler to go out over the next week.

To grow my social media presence over time I will:

_____

_____

_____

_____

☐ My Launch Team is in place

☐ I have communicated all of my launch plans to my launch team and they have access to assets to spread the word.

My plan for spreading the word about my podcast consists of:

_____

_____

_____

The
LAUNCH PHASE

"The price of success is hard work, dedication to the job at hand, and the determination that whether we win or lose, we have applied the best of ourselves to the task at hand."

— *Vince Lombardi*

DAY 45
Upload and Publish First 3 Episodes

You made it to the final phase! Now, it's time for launch.

Before you can submit your RSS feed to iTunes you have to have at least 1 episode published, and because we recommend launching with 3 episodes, it's time to get those uploaded and published!

Here's an 8-step podcast workflow to help you make sure your episodes are ready to go:

The 8-step podcast workflow

Step 1: Record

Step 2: Edit

Step 3: Add intro/outro

Step 4: Export

Step 5: Tag MP3

Step 6: Upload

Step 7: Schedule

Step 8: Publish

We recommend publishing your 3 episodes on the same day, about 30 minutes apart from one another (so they stay in the order you want them in).

We schedule the release of each of our episodes for 12:30 a.m. Eastern Time, which ensures they're ready and available first thing in the morning. You can choose any release time, and this might vary based on the time zone you're in.

EXERCISE:
Upload and Publish for Launch

⏱ Set a timer for 30 minutes

Upload and schedule your first 3 episodes in your media host. While completing this step, do a review of your media host settings to make sure everything is set up correctly.

Notes on uploading and publishing my episodes:

_____
_____
_____
_____
_____
_____
_____
_____
_____
_____
_____
_____

DAY 46
Submitting Your RSS Feed

Today is the day! You're ready to submit your RSS Feed to iTunes, Stitcher Radio, and any other distribution channels you're interested in.

EXERCISE:
Submit to iTunes

⏱ **Set a timer for 15 minutes**

1. Go to itunesconnect.apple.com
2. Login with your Apple ID and password (or create a new one if you don't already have one)
3. Once logged in, click on "My Podcasts"
4. Enter your RSS Feed (from your media host) and click on "validate"
5. Once validated, click "Submit"

iTunes can take anywhere from 24–72 hours to approve your podcast.

EXERCISE:
Submit to Stitcher Radio

⏱ **Set a timer for 15 minutes**

1. Go to Stitcher.com/content-providers
2. Log in with your username and password (or create a new one if you don't already have one)

3. Once logged in, click on "Partner Portal"

4. Follow the steps on the screen to submit your RSS feed

Congratulations on submitting your podcast!

DAY 47
Gaining Early Momentum

Gaining early momentum for your podcast is a combination of everything we've already covered, plus a marketing strategy that puts you in as many places as possible post-launch.

Some ideas for how you could "be everywhere" during your podcast launch and the weeks that follow:

- Send out a launch announcement to family, friends, your already-existing audience, and to your launch team;
- Set up guest podcast appearances on other podcasts in your industry/niche that will go live around the same time you launch;
- Request to guest post on blogs in your industry/niche that will be published around the same time you launch (and ideally lead people back to your site and podcast);
- Be present in the online communities where you know your avatar is hanging out—and provide as much value there as possible;
- Attend meetups and events where you'll be surrounded by your ideal listeners and can share your podcast if/when it makes sense;
- Put together a social media sharing strategy that is a combination of sharing others' content, in addition to sharing your own content;
- The list goes on!

Be creative! This is your podcast, and gaining early momentum will be important moving forward. There are dozens of things you can do to make sure your launch results in a big bang, and the above are just a few of those things.

EXERCISE:
Gaining Early Momentum

🕐 **Set a timer for 20 minutes**

List at least 5 strategies you'll use to help you gain early momentum:

1. _____
2. _____
3. _____
4. _____
5. _____

Now, put a plan in place and schedule specific times in your calendar when you'll implement these strategies.

My plan for gaining early momentum:

_____
_____
_____
_____
_____
_____
_____
_____
_____
_____
_____
_____
_____
_____
_____

DAY 48
Subscribe, Rate, and Review

Subscribe, Rate and Review are three magic words you should use over and over again throughout your podcasting journey.

The reason they're so magical:

- Subscribers will automatically get updates about your podcast and your new episodes delivered straight to their listening device;
- Ratings and Reviews will help potential new listeners figure out if your podcast is for them;
- The more subscribers and Ratings and Reviews you have, the more likely iTunes is to recognize your podcast.

EXERCISE:
Asking for Subscribers and Ratings and Reviews

⏱ **Set a timer for 30 minutes**

Create a short video tutorial you can direct people to where you walk through how to subscribe to your podcast and leave a Rating and Review.

You can use a tool like Loom or ScreenFlow to create your Subscribe, Rate and Review tutorial.

Once you've recorded your tutorial, create an email template asking your friends, family, and existing audience to subscribe to your podcast, and if they enjoy it, to leave a Rating and Review.

DAY 49
Ongoing Promotions Checklist

You've already set up the individual pieces that will contribute to your overall promotional strategy, and now it's time to make sure you have a handy checklist that can help you accomplish this every time you create a new episode.

Examples of things that might be included in your ongoing promotions checklist:

- Create a quick link to your episode (for example, yourwebsite.com/episode12 so your listeners can quickly and easily get to your show notes page)
- Create an image to share on social media
- Schedule and upload social media posts for the next week
- Create quick sharing links for Twitter (a Click To Tweet link)
- Email guests to let them know their episode is going live (include link to show notes, direct download link, episode image, and social sharing links)

EXERCISE:
Your Ongoing Promotions Checklist

 Set a timer for 15 minutes

Now it's your turn!

My ongoing promotions checklist:

- ☐ _____
- ☐ _____
- ☐ _____
- ☐ _____
- ☐ _____
- ☐ _____
- ☐ _____
- ☐ _____
- ☐ _____

DAY 50
Schedule Your 1-Month Podcast Review

Today you'll schedule your 1-month podcast review!

On Day 39 you set your podcast launch goal, along with your 1-, 3-, and 6-month goals. During your 1-month review time you're going to look back at your goals and gauge your progress.

When you do your 1-month review, ask yourself these questions:

What's working well for my podcast?

_____

_____

_____

What's not working well for my podcast?

_____

_____

_____

What are potential solutions to the things that aren't working well?

_____

_____

_____

What's one thing I can do right now to improve my podcast?

_____

_____

_____

What do I love most about my podcast?

_____

_____

_____

BEYOND

" Be undeniably good. No marketing effort or social media buzzword can be a substitute for that. "

— *Anthony Volodkin*

BONUS
Join Podcasters' Paradise

Throughout *The Podcast Journal* you've probably come up against struggles, things you had questions about, and ideas you'd love to get feedback on.

Having a community of like-minded people who know what you're going through and who can relate to the struggles and frustrations you face will make all the difference on your podcasting journey.

This is why we created Podcasters' Paradise, the #1 online podcasting community—period.

In addition to having a community of like-minded people, we've also created every resource you need to continue to be successful on your podcasting journey, including strategies for how to grow and monetize your podcast.

If you're looking for the step-by-step video tutorials, resources, email templates, and the documents you need to grow and monetize your podcast, then Podcasters' Paradise is for you.

Join us on our next Live Podcast Masterclass for a review of everything we've covered here, PLUS a behind-the-scenes look at Podcasters' Paradise, the #1 community for podcasters.

With over 3,000 members and growing, there's no better place to surround yourself with like-minded people, receive and give support, and learn the best tactics and strategies to create, grow, and monetize your podcast.

Claim your spot on our next live Masterclass and learn more about Paradise at PodcastersParadise.com!

Notes

Notes

Notes

Notes

Notes

Notes

Notes

Notes

Notes

Notes